THE CLAN O'BYRNE
OF LEINSTER
AD 400–1700

The Clan O'Byrne of Leinster

AD 400–1700

A Compilation of
Available Historical Information

PAUL J. BURNS

British Cataloguing in Publication Data
A catalogue record for this book is available
from the British Library

ISBN 1 899863 83 4

Typeset by XL Publishing Services, Tiverton.
Printed in Great Britain by SRP Ltd, Exeter
for House of Lochar, Isle of Colonsay, Argyll PA61 7YR

CONTENTS

PREFACE

Most Americans engaged in genealogical research of their Irish antecedents are content with tracing the ancestor who migrated from Ireland back to his point of origin. Few researchers have reason or, for that matter, the tools to work back further than the nineteenth century. There are numerous general histories of Ireland which provide the highlights of earlier times, but there has been surprisingly little compilation of materials on the individual tribes, or families.

While attempting to trace my particular Burns family back through the centuries to verify oral tradition, which has us descendent from the clan O'Byrne of the Wicklow Mountains, I found that I had opened a door to a thousand years of Irish history in which the clan O'Byrne had played a prominent role. References to the clan are scattered throughout many primary and secondary sources, but the few earlier attempts to summarize the clan's history are incomplete and inaccurate. There is little mention of the clan's earlier and quite fascinating history when, as the Ui Faelain, it was one of the most important of the Leinster tribes, provided eleven kings of Leinster, and was instrumental in preventing Brian Boru from establishing his dominance over all Ireland.

In the hopes that others of Irish descent with surnames Burns or Byrne will benefit from my research, I have compiled these notes on the history of the clan O'Byrne from its earliest recorded days until its dissolution in the seventeenth century.[1] This may make difficult reading for those not versed in Irish history, and there are many gaps yet unfilled; but, hopefully, it will provide some historical glimpses into the development and later eclipse of this once great Leinster clan.

A word of caution: not everyone with the surname Byrne

---

1. Among other spelling variations which occur in source materials are Beirne, Bern, Berne, Bhroin, Birn, Birne, Bourne, Bournes, Broin, Burn, Burne, Burnes, and Byrnes.

or one of its derivatives is descendent from the Leinster clan O'Byrne. An appendix contains some notes on other possible origins.

To prepare the scene: the Irish surname Burns stems from the name O'Byrne, which in its Gaelic form was Ua Broin or O Broin, meaning "descendant of Bran." Bran was an eleventh century chief of the Ui Faelain, as our tribe had been called since the eighth century. His name became our surname for no special reason other than that he was chief about the time when the usage of surnames began. Previously, tribal members were known by their own name plus that of their father and sometimes of their grandfather. Thus, Bran MacFaelan MacMurcadh Ua Faelain (to invent a name) was Bran, son of Faelan, grandson of Murcadh, of the (tribe of) Ui Faelain. Ui Faelain was the tribal name of the O'Byrnes for four centuries. It began to fall into disuse following adoption of a surname and, more importantly, because soon thereafter the tribe was forced off the Kildare lands with which the Ui Faelain name had become associated.

And a last word on the spelling of Irish names: there is no standardized way. Feagh MacHugh also is Fiach McHugh. Or perhaps the reader would prefer Fiachaidh mac Aodha. Should a writer use the anglicized O'Donnell, or be a purist and spell it O Domhnaill? Kildare or Cildara? I have no knowledge of the Gaelic language, and I apologize for any inadvertent errors.

Paul J. Burns
Tallahassee, Florida
December 2000

CHAPTER 1

THE FIRST MILLENNIUM
Rise of the Ui Faelain

The clan O'Byrne can be traced back to about the year A.D. 400 when a Celtic tribe named the Ui Dunlainge migrated north from Ossory into Leinster. There are several theories about the origins of the Ui Dunlainge, any one of which is as good as the others. Mythology has the tribe descending from Heremon, who supposedly invaded Ireland from Spain about 2000 B.C., and perhaps he did; but there is growing evidence that most of the waves of Celt invaders arrived from Britain. Some believe that the name Leinster is derived from the Lleyn Peninsula in Wales.

The Ui Dunlainge moved north in Leinster until it came to the rich plains along the Liffey river. The tribe forced out others then resident in that area, and settled down on some of the richest lands in Ireland, where it prospered and grew.[1]

The days of Cuchulain and Ireland's other legendary heroes were past. Christianity was arriving in the names of St. Patrick, St. Columba, and Kildare's own St. Brigid. Pagan ways were being melded with the new faith, though the newer, kinder religion did not much change traditional Celtic life. One of Ulster's last pagan kings requested burial fully armed and in an upright position facing south, to keep eternal vigilance against his hated Leinster enemies. Ireland at the time was divided, roughly, into the kingdoms of Munster, Leinster, Connaught, Ulster, and Mide (or Meath). At one time Leinster had extended much further north encompassing Tara, the seat of the high kings, but the rise of the Southern Ui Neill of Mide pushed the Leinstermen south, and the Ui Dunlainge became Leinster's frontier tribe.

By the first quarter of the eighth century the tribe was

---

1. Alfred P. Smyth, *Celtic Leinster: Towards an Historical Geography of Early Irish Civilization A. D. 500–1600* (Dublin: Irish Academic Press, 1982), p. 66.

becoming unwieldy and when its chief, Murcadh Mor, died, the Ui Dunlainge was divided among his three sons to become the Ui Muiredaig, Ui Faelain, and Ui Dunchadha. Ireland at the time had no more than 250,000 inhabitants, of whom 40,000 were in Leinster. The Ui Dunlainge had numbered about 12,000. The Ui Faelain, named after Murcadh Mor's son Faelan, was the largest of the three divisions with, perhaps, 5,000 members. It could field about 700 warriors, a very large force for those days.[2]

The tribe occupied lands centering on present-day Naas in northern County Kildare, lands which corresponded to the baronies of North Naas, North and South Salt, Clane, Ikeathy and Outhternany, and portions of adjoining ones.[3] The Curragh of Kildare, of present-day horse breeding fame, belonged to the Ui Faelain (in 782 Ruaidhri, son of Faelan, defeated the chief of the Ui Muiredaig on the Curragh, the prize being both control of the Curragh and the kingship of Leinster),[4] as did, sporadically, a famous and wealthy monastery at Kildare. A brother of Faelan was the abbot of the monastery; but the Ui Faelain apparently did not control this rich prize continuously, as evidenced by the Ui Faelain's plunderings of the monastery in 831, 1022, and 1024.[5]

Though they often fought each other the Ui Faelain, Ui Muiredaig, and Ui Dunchadha remained loosely linked by historical ties, intermarriage, and politics in what historians call the Ui Dunlainge confederacy. Between them they controlled the throne of Leinster for many centuries. On occasion the more powerful Ui Neill from Ulster would impose a king from another Leinster tribe, but these times were rare. The Ui Faelain was the largest of the three tribes in the Ui Dunlainge confederacy and controlled Naas, the

2. Ibid., p. 5.
3. John Edge, *The O'Byrnes and Their Descendants* (Dublin: Porteous and Gibbs, 1879), pp. 10–11.
4. Smyth, p. 128.
5. *The Annals of the Kingdom of Ireland, by the Four Masters*, ed. John O'Donovan (Dublin: 1848–1871). Hereafter cited as *Four Masters* with chronological date instead of page.

seat of Leinster kings. Despite this, the three observed a rough rotation of the Leinster throne.[6]

The Annals of the Kingdom of Ireland by the Four Masters, compiled in the seventeenth century, first mentions the Ui Faelain as a tribe in an entry for the year 837 when "Bran, son of Faelan, from whom is named Ui Faelain, died." A footnote says that this was the name of a tribe in the plains of Magh-Liffe and Magh-Laighean in the north of present-day County Kildare. This area also was called Airthir-Life (eastern Liffey).

Early references to the Ui Faelain by the Four Masters usually concerned someone's death, since battles were frequent and male life expectancy short in those "heroic" times. When a later Faelan, king of Leinster, died of a fall on the Curragh in 940, his non-battle death was unusual enough for a special eulogy by the Four Masters:

> "Faelan of resounding rapidity, whose shout
>   overwhelmed the plain,
> Lord of Cualann of the harbors (Dublin), the subduer of
>   champions, king of Leinster,
> The flame of Heremon's Ireland, he subdued hosts
>   single handed,
> Cause of tears in his total separation, Alas for the Prince
>   of Faelan's land (Ui Faelain)"

The infrequent glimpses of tribal activity show that, confederacy or not, there were frequent disputes with the Ui Muiredaig and Ui Dunchadha, as well as raids on various monasteries, war against the Ui Neill to the north, and battles with other tribes to the south and west. The most frequent mentions of all concern the Norsemen, or Ostmen, who settled in Dublin. Ui Faelain lands were little more than 20 miles from Ath-Cliath, as Dublin was called, so raids and battles were frequent. In 861 an Ui Faelain chief named Muiregan was killed by Norsemen; in 915 Muiregan's son

6. Smyth, p. 123.

Maelmordha was killed by them; in 941 Lorcan, king of
Leinster and the Ui Faelain, was slain "while plundering Ath-
Cliath"; and in 942 the Ui Faelain and other tribes completely
destroyed the Norse settlement. On the other hand, the Ui
Faelain was not always at war with the Norsemen, and the
two were often allies. In time, the Norse settlers became
regarded as another tribe, to be plundered when weak and
as potential allies when strong.[7]

7. *Four Masters*, 861, 915, 941, 942.

CHAPTER 2

THE ELEVENTH CENTURY
Troubles with Brian

For three centuries the Ui Faelain had provided about one-third of the kings of Leinster, the Ui Muiredaig and Ui Dunchadha sharing equally in the remainder. Maelmordha, chief of the Ui Faelain, was king of Leinster when Brian Borumha, chief of the Dal Cais tribe and king of Munster, attempted to conquer Ireland. Brian Borumha is better known to history as Brian Boru.[1]

An especially interesting character in the Ui Faelain's history was Gormlaith, Maelmordha's sister, whom he married to Olaf Ironshoe, the Norse king of Dublin. Olaf and Gormlaith produced Sitric Silkbeard and, when Sitric was grown, Olaf abdicated in his favor to enter a monastery.[2] Many historians believe that he was fleeing from his strong-willed wife, Gormlaith, who was too much for even a Viking to handle. Gormlaith then married Maelseachlainn of the Southern Ui Neill, who was king of Meath and high king (Ard Ri) of Ireland. The high king was a largely honorary position usually alternated between the Northern and Southern Ui Neill, but it was Brian Boru's goal. Gormlaith was too much for Maelseachlainn as well, because she next appeared as the second (or third) wife of Brian Boru, who may have mistakenly thought that he could build a relationship with the Norsemen and with the king of Leinster through her. She became estranged from Brian Boru and was living with Sitric, her son, at the time of the battle of Clontarf. Gormlaith appears in the Njals Saga of Iceland as a beautiful but grim and scheming lady who plays one man off against

1. Brian obtained the name Borumha, pronounced Boru and meaning cattle, by reimposing an ancient cattle tax on Leinster. Northern kings had originated this levy but dropped it after centuries of Leinster uprisings in protest.
2. James Charles Roy, *The Road Wet, The Wind Close* (Dublin: Gill and Macmillan, 1986), pp. 188–89.

another in ruthless quest for vengeance against Brian Boru.[3]

In the year 999 Brian Boru had defeated the combined forces of Leinster and the Norsemen in battle, following which Maelseachlainn stepped down in his favor as high king. Brian's scheme to unify the island probably never would have worked simply because he already was elderly, and the one hundred Celtic tribes then existent were centuries removed from any concept of nationhood. The Leinster tribes under Maelmordha viewed him as an invader from Munster, and in 1014 they rose against him supported by the Norsemen of Dublin, who brought in reinforcements from the Orkneys and Hebrides. Gormlaith was instrumental in provoking the war. She had ridiculed her brother Maelmordha for having submitted to Brian,[4] and she helped forge an alliance between Maelmordha and her son Sitric of Dublin. Sitric, probably with Gormlaith's connivance, enlisted the support of two Viking chiefs of the Hebrides and the Orkneys by promising each, separately, Gormlaith's hand in marriage. A great battle was fought at Clontarf, now a suburb of Dublin, by Brian's army of Munstermen, Connaughtmen, and Cork and Limerick Vikings, against Maelmordha and Sitric's army of Leinstermen, Dublin Vikings, and imported Vikings from the Orkneys and the Hebrides.[5] The Meath king, Maelseachlainn, and the Ulster tribes were conspicuously absent from the battle.[6] Although Brian's army won, his victory was Pyrrhic, and the true winner was Maelseachlainn. Both Brian Boru and Maelmordha were killed in the battle, and Maelseachlainn resumed the office of high king.[7]

Gormlaith, daughter of one king, sister of another, wife of

3. *Njal's Saga*, trans. Carl F. Bayerschmidt and Lee M. Hollander (New York: Greenwood Press, 1955), pp. 352–53.
4. John Ryan, "The Battle of Clontarf," *The Journal of The Royal Society of Antiquaries of Ireland* (1938), p. 6.
5. *The War of the Gaedhil with the Gaill, or the Invasion of Ireland by the Danes and other Norsemen*, trans. James H. Todd (London: 1867), p. 142 ff.
6. Ryan believes Maelseachlainn and his Meathmen fought on Brian's side at Clontarf. Other authorities disagree.
7. *Njal's*, pp. 352–353.

three, and mother of two – Sitric of Dublin and Donnchadha of Munster (her son by Brian Boru) – lived on until 1030, but no man brave enough to be her fourth husband appeared. An ancient poem read:

"Gormlaith took three leaps,
 Which a woman never shall again,
 A leap at Ath-Cliath, a leap at Teamhair,
 A leap at Caiseal of the goblets over all." [8]

Ath-Cliath was Dublin, Teamhair was another name for Tara, and Caiseal was Cashel, the seat of the Munster kings.

The last of the Ui Faelain to serve as king of Leinster was Maelmordha's son Braen, or Bran, whose reign was short. He was deposed by the Ui Neill about 1016, presumably by Maelseachlainn seeking revenge against an Ui Faelain weakened by losses at Clontarf, and the chief of the Ui Muiredaig was placed on the throne. It was this Bran from whom the O Broin, later the O'Byrnes, took their name. Bran later was blinded by Sitric Silkbeard, his first cousin,[9] it being an old Irish custom to blind rivals to prevent them from holding office. Only warriors without physical blemish could be tribal chief or king.

The death of Brian Boru ended the impossible dream of a united Ireland, and the one hundred tribes happily went back to warring against each other. In 1019 the Ui Faelain raided the abbey of Clonard in Meath, and in 1022 they plundered the monastery of Kildare. The Ui Failghe, a tribe to the west, apparently had regained control of it. Two years later Donnsleibhe, chief of the Ui Faelain, was slain by the Ui Failghe at Kildare, having returned to plunder the monastery once again.[10] The following decades saw many such raids against the Ui Failghe to the west, the Fortuatha to the east, against the related Ui Muiredaig to the south and Ui Dunchadha to the northeast....

8. *Four Masters*, 1030.
9. *Four Masters*, footnote to 1052.
10. *Four Masters*, 1019, 1022, 1024.

There are almost no references to the Ui Faelain in the Four Masters for the last half of the eleventh century, though the tribe could hardly have been inactive. Occupying some of the richest lands in Ireland, strategically located near the Norsemen of Dublin, and close to the border of the kingdom of Meath, the Ui Faelain had to fight constantly to survive.

CHAPTER 3

THE TWELFTH CENTURY
The Norman Conquest

Two related events were to occur in the twelfth century which drastically changed the course of Irish history, as well as the fortunes of the Ui Faelain. These were the rise to power in Leinster of a rival confederation, and the invitation by a deposed chief of this confederation to the Normans to invade Ireland. To go back in time, when the Ui Dunlainge invaded Leinster from Ossory in the fifth century, it was accompanied by a related tribe, the Ui Cheinnselaig. The routes of the tribes diverged in Leinster, the Ui Dunlainge migrating north toward Kildare, and the Ui Cheinnselaig turning east to settle in Wexford and Carlow.[1] It, too, grew and divided into several tribes which remained linked into an Ui Cheinnselaig confederation. By the eleventh century this south Leinster confederation had grown strong enough to challenge the northern Ui Dunlainge confederation for dominance of the kingdom itself. The Ui Cheinnselaig did not support the king of Leinster, Maelmordha of the Ui Faelain, at the battle of Clontarf. Because the northern tribes suffered heavy casualties at that battle, the balance of power in Leinster shifted to the southern confederation, and from 1042 onwards all Leinster kings came from the Ui Chiennselaig.

In 1126 Diarmaid Mac Murchadha,[2] lord of the Ui Cheinneslaig confederation, became king of Leinster. He solidified his position by killing Domhnall Mac Fhaelain, chief of the Ui Faelain, killing the head of the Ui Muiredaig clan and, in 1141, blinding sixteen other Leinster chieftains to remove them as potential rivals.[3] Mac Murchadha, from whom the Kavanaghs descend, was guilty of many other unsavory actions. For example, he sent men to rape the

1. Smyth, p. 66.
2. Anglicized Dermot MacMurrough.
3. *Four Masters*, 1141.

abbess of Kildare, who was from the Ui Faelain, because only a virgin could be abbess.

In 1153 there was a large battle in Westmeath between Mac Murchadha's Leinster forces and the Ui Neill, which the latter won. To weaken Mac Murchadha, the Ui Neill took hostages from the Ui Faelain, and transferred control of the tribe and its lands to the king of Meath. In 1167 Donnchadha, chief of the Ui Faelain, led 2,000 Ui Faelain cavalry to a large gathering of the tribes in Meath, called the Convention of Trachta.[4] The Ui Faelain were still subservient at that time to the king of Meath.

Mac Murchadha's ambition was to become high king of Ireland, and his constant scheming eventually caused his downfall. In 1166 the northern Leinster tribes rose against him supported by Meath and the Dublin Norsemen. Mac Murchadha was defeated and banished from Ireland. He spent three years in England and on the continent seeking support to regain his throne, and he eventually obtained the help he sought by betraying his country. Mac Murchadha made promises to several Norman lords in Wales which were far beyond the powers of any Irish ruler to keep. For instance, he promised the Norman leader "Strongbow"[5] that he would inherit the throne of Leinster by virtue of marriage to Mac Murchadha's daughter. This was meaningless to the Irish, whose custom was to elect their kings and chiefs. Leadership was not automatically inherited.[6]

The Normans first landed in 1169, and two years later they were raiding the territories of the Ui Faelain. Mac Murchadha had reclaimed the tribe and its lands for his kingdom of Leinster, and his desire for revenge was especially strong against Faelan Mac Fhaelain, lord of the Ui Faelain, for his role in Mac Murchadha's earlier banishment. Mac

---

4. *Four Masters*, 1167.
5. Richard de Clare, Earl of Pembroke, was called Strongbow although this actually was his father's nickname.
6. To avoid succession disputes, the English used the system of primogeniture. Celtic kings were elected, although selection was usually limited to a royal family. The royal heir, or "Tanist," also was elected, and all too often his impatience for the throne caused instability.

Murchadha died in 1171, and Strongbow claimed his throne.

Mac Murchadha's death and Strongbow's claim to the throne of Leinster were the signals for the tribes to rise against the invaders. Rory O'Conor, the high king, with Murchad Mac Murchadha, Diarmaid's own brother who rejected Strongbow's claim to the Leinster throne, and Faelan Mac Fhaelain, king of the Ui Faelain,[7] joined forces to besiege the Normans in Dublin. The Ui Donchadha and the Ui Muiredaig also participated. After several weeks of watching for their moment, heavily armored Normans sallied forth to catch the less disciplined Irish off guard, and the siege was broken with heavy losses to the besiegers.[8]

On an excursion south from Dublin, Strongbow captured Murrough O'Brain and his son, who had deserted Mac Murchadha in 1166. The O'Brains of the Duffry, as they were called, were a minor branch of the Ui Faelain whom Mac Murchadha had moved south to guard a vulnerable pass into Leinster from Ossory.[9] Once captured, they were beheaded and their bodies thrown to the dogs.[10]

Historians say that the Ui Faelain were dispossessed of their Kildare lands in the year 1203, but this is an error based on a footnote in the Four Masters. An entry for 1203 concerning the death of Faelan Mac Fhaelain is footnoted with a description of the tribe's holdings in Kildare "from which it was driven shortly after the English invasion." It is clear, however, that the O'Tooles[11] were forced from their lands in 1178, and it is probable that the O'Byrnes would

7. The Mac Fhaelains were the royal family of the Ui Faelain during this century. The Mac Fhaelains did not accompany the rest of the tribe in the migration to the Wicklow Mountains, probably because the royal family was in hostage to the Normans. Faelan Mac Fhaelain entered a monastery shortly after this time, and the Mac Fhaelain line appears to have died out.
8. Goddard Henry Orpen, *Ireland Under the Normans, 1169–1216* (Oxford: Clarendon Press, 1968), I, p. 161.
9. T. W. Moody, F. X. Martin and F. J. Byrne, eds. *A New History of Ireland* (Oxford: 1976-1984), II, 28, 63.
10. Orpen, I, p. 237.
11. The Ui Muiredaig became known as the O Tuatthail, or O'Tooles, after their migration to the Wicklows.

have been driven away at the same time. When Strongbow died in 1176 his will divided Kildare into "Offelan," "Offaly," and "OMurethy." Offelan (Ui Faelain) contained three "cantreds."[12] Carbury, the cantred furthest from Dublin, was willed to Meiler Fitz Henry; the middle cantred, which included Naas, was given to Maurice Fitz Gerald; and the cantred nearest Dublin went to Adam de Hereford who divided it with his brothers, John and Richard. These Norman worthies would have acted long before 1203 to occupy their new lands.[13]

The warlike Ui Faelain and Ui Muiredaig would not have left without heavy fighting, and casualties must have been high. Still, enough survived to migrate east to the more defensible Wicklow mountains where weaker tribes – the Ui Briuin Chualan, Ui Enechglaiss, and the Dal Messin Corb – were driven out. Ironically, these were the very same tribes which the Ui Dunlainge drove out of Kildare centuries before.

The Ui Muiredaig, now the O'Tooles, occupied the northern and western slopes of the Wicklow Mountains. The Ui Faelain, now the O'Byrnes, occupied the eastern and southern slopes. The senior branch of the O'Byrnes held the coastal lands from present-day Delgany on the north to Arklow on the south, between the sea and the River Varty. This territory was called Crioch Branach, or O'Byrnes land. The junior branch settled in the less desirable mountain lands from the River Varty west to the border of County Carlow near Shillelagh, with seat at Ballinacor in the Glenmalure valley. Its lands were called Gabhal Raghnuill.[14,15]

---

12. A cantred was a medieval land division similar in size to a barony.
13. Orpen, I, 377–81.
14. *Leabhar Branach: Or the Book of the O'Byrnes*, ed. Sean Mac Airt (Dublin: The Dublin Institute for Advanced Studies, 1944), p. ix.
15. It is not clear whether the junior and senior branches were distinct before the move to the Wicklows, or whether the division resulted from geographic separation once there.

CHAPTER 4

THE THIRTEENTH CENTURY
The Mountain Fastness

During the late twelfth and early thirteenth centuries the Normans conquered and distributed among themselves large portions of Ireland, but they were not able to subjugate the entire island. Wars on the continent diverted much of their attention, and they still were not completely in control of Britain. The initial invasion of Ireland was not, in fact, carried out by that neighboring nation; it was mostly the work of a handful of Norman lords whom the English/Norman king did not fully trust, although he had authorized their action. The early success of the Normans in Ireland was not due to their numbers, but rather to their more efficient war tactics – armored knights, coordinated battle maneuvers, and archers – none of which was used by the Irish Celts of the time. Celtic emphasis was on individual bravery, so that a battle between Irish forces was a mass contest between pairs of dueling warriors armed with hand weapons such as swords and axes. The Irish considered the use of archers to be cowardly, and did not have a much higher opinion of armor. Warriors worked themselves into a frenzy before battle, and they sometimes tore off what little protective clothing they had to charge the enemy naked. They did use horses, but primarily to carry the warriors to the battle scene. In time they learned to make use of mountains and bogs to thwart armored knights, and thick forest to counter archers. The difficult topography of the Wicklows was the greatest ally of the O'Byrnes and O'Tooles in delaying the English conquest of their lands for the next several centuries.

The Four Masters do not mention the Ui Faelain, now the O'Byrnes, during their entire chronology for the thirteenth century. One must turn instead to English historical documents where the first mention of the tribe concerns the year 1271. This of course leaves almost a hundred year gap in this narrative. One supposes that during this time the

O'Byrnes were recuperating from decimation at the hands of the Normans, warring against the lesser tribes whom they were pushing out of their chosen area, and consolidating their hold on their new "sword lands".[1]

A.J. Otway-Ruthven's *A History of Medieval Ireland* first mentions these former Kildare but now Wicklow tribes in describing the problems of the king's newly appointed justiciar (chief representative in Ireland) in 1271 with the terse comment, "activity against the O'Byrnes and O'Tooles."[2] Two years later another justiciar faced the same problem and, despite serious troubles in Connaught, he considered the most immediate priority to be pacification of the mountain areas of Wicklow, so close to the English seat at Dublin. The entire Wicklow area supposedly belonged to the king himself, so these developing raids by tribes living on the king's claimed lands against the king's estates in the surrounding lowlands were especially painful. In 1274 a force under this justiciar, Geoffrey de Greneville, was defeated at Glenmalure – far from the last time the English were to hear of that mountain valley – with heavy losses in slain and prisoners, and De Greneville was wounded. The following year another attempt was made against Glenmalure, but it also was unsuccessful. In 1276 De Greneville led a third attack on Glenmalure and, again, his army of over 2,000 soldiers, very large for the times, was defeated with heavy losses. In 1277 yet a fourth attack was attempted, and this one is said to have been more successful.[3] War flared again in 1294, and in 1295 Maurice MacMurrough (formerly Mac Murchadha),[4] acting as king of unconquered Leinster, gave hostages from the O'Byrnes, O'Tooles, and Kavanaghs, and promised to keep them peaceful. This was to be short-lived.[5]

1. Orpen, II, 133; IV, 8–20.
2. A.J. Otway-Ruthven, *A History of Medieval Ireland* (New York: St. Martin's Press, 1968), p. 200.
3. Otway-Ruthven, pp. 201–02.
4. The Mac Murchadhas became first the MacMurroughs and then the Kavanaghs, a name derived from an illegitimate son of Diarmaid Mac Murchadha.
5. Otway-Ruthven, p. 212. Also, Orpen, IV, 8–20.

CHAPTER 5

THE FOURTEENTH CENTURY
Guerrilla Warfare

The Four Masters again provide almost no information on the O'Byrnes during the 1300s, the only mention being a footnote to the year 1369 which says that one Thomas O'Birn died.[1] But English documents provide frequent mention. At the beginning of the century English control of Ireland was weak, and slipping. The king's justiciar and other lords were summoned to fight in Scotland, and the Irish of the mountains immediately rose up. Early in 1302 the English sent an expedition to north Wexford "to repress the rebellion of the MacMurroughs and O'Byrnes."[2] In 1308 and 1309 there was much fighting around Glendalough in the Wicklow mountains and in north Wexford, according to documents concerning the rebellion of one Maurice de Caunteton, who led other Anglo-Irish families such as the Harolds and Archibolds and, in alliance with Dunlang O'Byrne and other Leinster Irish, rose up against the king.[3] De Caunteton was soon killed but the war raged on. In 1311 the O'Byrnes were again (still?) at war, burning and plundering the king's estates at Rathcoole and Saggart.[4]

The war in Scotland had much effect in Ireland. Edward, the brother of Robert the Bruce, landed in Ulster in May 1315 to foment an uprising against the English. The Irish of the Wicklows immediately joined him against the common enemy, as did many of the other clans. Edward led his army south into Leinster, then returned to Ulster. The English of Dublin were unable to pursue him because they were busy combatting the uprisings of the Leinster tribes. In December

---

1. This Thomas was not head of the junior or senior branch. He may have been head of a branch which became extinct.
2. Otway-Ruthven, p. 218.
3. Ibid., p. 219.
4. Moody, II, 279.

1316 Robert the Bruce joined Edward to lead an army south through Leinster to Limerick, returning to Ulster through Kildare. Again, the English were too weak to pursue, in large part because of the depredations of the O'Byrnes and O'Tooles, who plundered the coastal towns in Wicklow.[5]

Robert Bruce returned to Scotland, but in October 1318 Edward, who had declared himself king of Ulster, attempted once more to invade the south, only to be killed at Dundalk. The three and a half years of war had caused much famine and left the English greatly weakened. A report sent to the king in 1320 said that much of the king's lands in south County Dublin (now County Wicklow) had been "invaded, burned, and totally devastated by the Irish of the mountains."[6]

There was no let up, however, despite the disappearance of the Scots from the scene. A major preoccupation of the king's justiciar was the now endemic warfare with the Wicklow Mountains tribes, and in 1324 he raised an army to combat the "McMurghuthys and Obrynnes" (Mac-Murroughs and O'Byrnes). This apparently was not successful, because the next summer it was necessary to post guards against them at Baltinglass and Dunlavan.[7] In 1328 the Leinster clans met and chose a king, Donnell MacMurrough, but he and the chief of the O'Tooles were soon captured (O'Toole was executed but MacMurrough later escaped). Their capture had little effect on the other tribes and, in August and again in December 1329, the justiciar led expeditions against the O'Byrnes.[8] In other campaigns the English forces put down the O'Mores, O'Dempseys, O'Nolans, and MacGeoghegans; but

---

5. Otway-Ruthven, p. 219.
6. Orpen, IV, 179.
7. Otway-Ruthven, p. 242.
8. Orpen, IV, 229–30. The August expedition consisted of 78 men-at-arms, 291 hobelers, and 285 footmen, while the December effort contained 77 men-at-arms, 240 hobelers, and 65 footmen. A hobeler was a light-horseman.

campaigns against the O'Byrnes and other mountain tribes had limited success.[9]

A few years of relative peace followed, but in 1334 the O'Byrnes and other mountain tribes were once again harassing the English settlements, while the king's justiciar was busy in Connaught. Continuous warfare had laid waste much of Ireland. The total population was less than one million; levies of Irish soldiers to fight in Scotland went unfilled; and English landlords complained of a shortage of tenants. The Wicklow tribes were not at all bothered by levies or wastelands, being very much responsible for much of the latter, but the continuous warfare must have taken a heavy toll on the O'Byrnes, O'Tooles, and MacMurroughs (Kavanaghs). Many centuries later a writer named O'Toole speculated that the reason there are so many more Byrnes in the world today than O'Tooles is because the O'Tooles were closer to Dublin and bore the brunt of English attacks. This may be partly true, but the Ui Faelain was a much larger tribe than the Ui Muiredaig and could absorb more casualties.[10]

Times of peace were at best intermittent. There was another campaign against the O'Byrnes in the summer of 1342, and in 1346 an English report complained that the Irish of Leinster continued at war with the English "burning, spoiling, and killing whom they can."[11]

Two years later the plague reached Ireland, decimating the cities where the English were concentrated. The mountain isolation of the Wicklow tribes spared them the worst horrors of the Black Death, which was to return in 1361 and 1371.

Another campaign against the O'Byrnes in 1350 apparently met with some success. Later that year the tribe elected its chief in the presence of the king's justiciar, Thomas de Rokeby, a veteran of the wars in Scotland who, by recognizing John O'Byrne as captain-elect of his nation,

9. Otway-Ruthven, pp. 246-47.
10. P. L. O'Toole, "The History of the Clan O'Byrne (Ui Faelan)," *History of the Clan O'Toole and Other Leinster Septs* (Dublin: 1890), p. 5.
11. Otway-Ruthven, p. 258.

bestowed some legality on him.[12] As always, peace was short-lived, and there was a campaign against the O'Byrnes in September and October 1353, and yet another in 1354. Frantic messages for reinforcements and help for numerous wounded imply that the justiciar's army was badly mauled in the latter campaign. In April 1355 the O'Byrnes again rose in war, and an August document complained of daily threats from them against the counties of Dublin, Kildare, Carlow, and Wexford, a great part of which they had already destroyed. There were campaigns against the O'Byrnes in 1357 and 1358. By May 1359 the English had achieved some success against the MacMurroughs, who gave hostages, but the O'Tooles and O'Byrnes were still at war. The following year, however, ten O'Byrnes were hostages in Dublin Castle.[13]

There may have been a few years of peace, but the rest of the century was to be a repetition of the earlier portion. History notes an English campaign against the O'Byrnes in 1364, against the Irish of Leinster in 1369 and 1370, the O'Byrnes burning a castle in 1373 and taking the constable prisoner, the Leinster tribes sacking the town of Carlow in 1377, and so on. The whole of Leinster seems to have been at war throughout that decade and into the 1380s.

The Wicklow mountains were not the only area of endemic unrest, of course, or they eventually would have been subjugated by sheer numbers. Troubles in Munster, Connaught, and Ulster often drew off the English forces and required sizeable garrisons. Still, poised as they were above Dublin and overlooking the fertile Liffey and Barrow valleys, the Wicklows were an important deterrent to English dominance, and the inability to put down the O'Tooles, O'Byrnes, and MacMurroughs caused many an English ulcer.

In 1386 the clans were again raiding the outskirts of Dublin; and in 1391 Carlow once more was burned and all

12. Edmund Curtis, *A History of Ireland* (London: Metheun & Co., 1936), p. 110.
13. Otway-Ruthven, pp. 280–84.

Kildare was "in flames." Expeditions against the O'Byrnes continued but achieved only limited and temporary success. Finally, however, England's wars in Scotland and on the continent ceased for a time, and King Richard II could turn his attention to Ireland. In September 1394 Richard made the crossing to lead an army of 8,000 against the tribes, an army comparable to that which fought against France. No fools, the Leinster tribal chiefs went to Dublin to submit to him, and Art MacMurrough Kavanagh, recognized by the tribes as their king, promised to keep them quiet in exchange for a pension and the return of his wife's Kildare lands. The king traveled south to Carlow where Gerald O'Byrne submitted to him, and Donal O'Byrne reaffirmed his earlier submission in Dublin.[14] Donal appears to have been "the O'Byrne", though the separate submission of Gerald would appear to mean that the junior and senior branches of the tribe already were operating separately. The tribes promised to quit Leinster and go elsewhere to fight for the king in his pay, promises which they made no attempt to keep.[15]

King Richard II went back to England and, needless to say, the Wicklow Irish again rose up. In July 1398 the O'Byrnes killed the king's justiciar Roger Mortimer, fourth Earl of March and seventh Earl of Ulster, in an engagement near Carlow.[16] Richard II was forced to return to Ireland with another army, and in 1399 he led an expedition north along the eastern slopes of the Wicklows through the heart of O'Byrne country. This was in defiance of an old Irish taboo against kings traveling in a counter-clockwise direction. The superstition may have been true because Richard met with disaster. His cavalry useless in the dense forests, stragglers picked off by hovering tribesmen, his army close to starvation, Richard barely made it back to Dublin. He returned to England to counter troubles there, only to be imprisoned and forced to abdicate in favor of his cousin, who became Henry IV.

14. Ibid., pp. 290–311.
15. Curtis, p. 128.
16. Otway-Ruthven, p. 336.

Though the Norman/English controlled many towns and manors in Leinster at the end of the century, the whole, wild interior was controlled by the O'Byrnes, O'Tooles, and allied tribes. The coast from Bray to Arklow was O'Byrne country, except for the castles of Wicklow and Newcastle.

CHAPTER 6

THE FIFTEENTH CENTURY
Beyond the Pale

With the departure of Richard, England's interests in Ireland were left in confusion. The new king, Henry IV, had too many other problems to pay much attention to his reluctant Hibernian subjects, and uprisings and raids continued. Histories associate many of these with MacMurrough, king of Leinster from the year 1400 on, and there were various English campaigns against him. The O'Byrnes had pledged peace to the king's justiciar in November 1401, but as usual this was short-lived. In 1405 the O'Byrnes burned Newcastle,[1] and it is probable that they were with MacMurrough on his Leinster raids throughout the decade. There is mention of an English expedition against the O'Byrnes in 1410,[2] during which some of the king's troops (probably Irish levies) deserted to the enemy, and in 1413 the O'Byrnes attacked Dublin itself.

In 1415 the king appointed Sir John Talbot justiciar and, more capable than most, he subdued many of the Irish tribes. There was little mention of the O'Byrnes during his six-year tenure, but he led many expeditions against MacMurrough, and it is probable that the O'Byrnes and O'Tooles were involved. Talbot captured MacMurrough (Donnchad Kavanagh) in 1419 and sent him to the Tower of London, but MacMurrough's brother Gerald became acting king of Leinster and carried on the resistance. There was a mention of the O'Byrnes in Talbot correspondence, circa 1420, in which Talbot accused his arch-enemy, the Duke of Ormond, of having been in alliance with the O'Byrnes when they attacked Wicklow Castle and murdered the king's constable.[3]

Ormond, who succeeded Talbot, was obviously more

1. Moody, VIII, chronology for 1405, 1413.
2. Otway-Ruthven, p. 346.
3. Ibid., p. 358.

acceptable to the Irish, because his term as justiciar, 1421–23, was relatively peaceful. Following his dismissal, however, there were numerous uprisings during which Gerald Kavanagh plundered Wexford, and the O'Tooles warred on Dublin and Kildare. The O'Byrnes must have been with these allied tribes, because in June 1423 the justiciar received messages from the O'Byrne and Kavanagh once again pledging peace, and in 1425 the O'Byrne submitted to him. Talbot became king's justiciar again later that year, and he was required to take vigorous action against the O'Byrnes. "Donat Obryn, captain of his nation," soon submitted, as did the O'Toole, and peace once again reigned, at least long enough for the fall harvest.[4]

In 1427 there was another change in justiciars, and the Irish of Leinster seized the opportunity to rise under MacMurrough, some 3,000 strong. The Irish forces burned towns in Kildare, drove the justiciar away from Naas, laid waste to Wexford, then returned to Kildare to take the walled town of Castledermot by assault. The involvement of the O'Byrnes was proven by a report which the justiciar sent to London defending his lack of success in putting down the uprising; in it he said that some of the Irish chiefs had joined him against the O'Byrnes.[5]

The next twenty years were especially turbulent, and English holdings were reduced to little more than a portion of County Dublin and a few walled towns. In 1442 the English of Dublin and Meath attacked O'Byrne country, but the O'Byrnes and O'Tooles overtook the returning forces, killed 80, and stripped them of "countless spoils."[6] At mid-century many portions of the country had not been visited by the justiciar in several decades, unless he was passing through with his army. Irish lords employed thousands of Scots mercenaries called "gallowglasses" to assist with the fighting, against each other if not against the English. The English achieved some success in 1449 when Richard, Duke

4. Ibid., pp. 363–64.
5. Otway-Ruthven, p. 366.
6. *Four Masters*, 1442.

of York, was appointed king's representative in Ireland. In July of that year Richard summoned all loyal forces to meet him on the Wicklow coast, with the apparent intention of subduing the mountain tribes. Instead, he marched north to pacify Ulster, following which, accompanied by the Ulster Irish, he marched south against the O'Byrnes. Their chief, Brian O'Byrne, submitted, promising to wear English clothing and learn the English language.[7]

Setbacks in the wars in France and the outbreak of the War of the Roses in England again diverted English attention from Ireland. Richard, the king's representative, was one of the principal protagonists of the English civil war, and he was forced to neglect his Irish duties. Richard was killed in battle in 1460, but his cause prevailed, and the following year his son became King Edward IV.

There was little change in Ireland. In 1463 an English army in Leinster was defeated by the O'Byrnes, in 1466 the justiciar led an expedition against the O'Byrnes, and in 1471 the O'Byrnes and O'Tooles again burned most of the town of Saggart in County Kildare.[8]

The Anglo-Irish remained strongly Yorkist during this complicated period in English history, but the tribes appear to have been divided. In 1487 some supported an impersonator backed by the Anglo-Irish as the true heir to the English throne, but the O'Byrnes were among those who asserted their loyalty to Henry VII, the first of the Tudors. It is doubtful that they cared who was king and, while not averse to a good fight, they preferred that it be about something more important to them.

7. Otway-Ruthven, p. 380, and Moody, II, 559.
8. Otway-Ruthven, pp. 390–95.

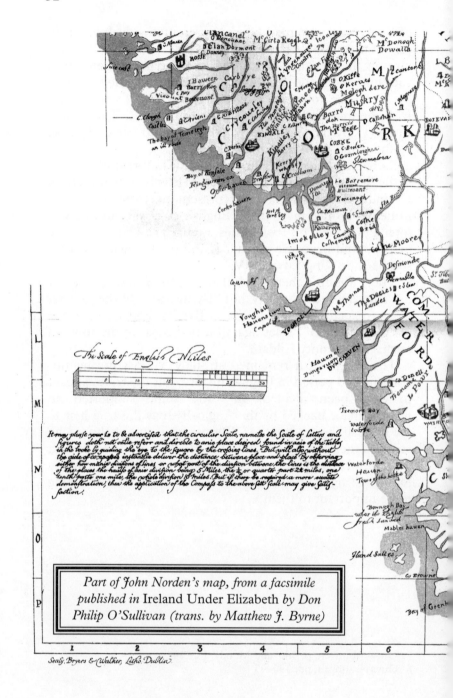

32

The Scale of English Miles

It may please your lo to be advertised, that the circular Scale, namelie the Scale of Letters and figures doth not onlie referr and directe to anie place desired found in anie of the tables in the booke by guiding the eye to the square by the crossing lines. But will also without the aide of compasses instantlie deliver the distance betwene place and place. By observing either how manie divisions of lines, or cutoff part of the division betwene the lines is the distance of the places the half plaine division being 5 Miles, the ¼, or quarter part 2½ miles, and tenth parte one mile; the whole division 10 miles. But if there be required a more secure demonstration; then the application of the Compass to the above sd Scale may give satisfaction.

Part of John Norden's map, from a facsimile published in Ireland Under Elizabeth by Don Philip O'Sullivan (trans. by Matthew J. Byrne)

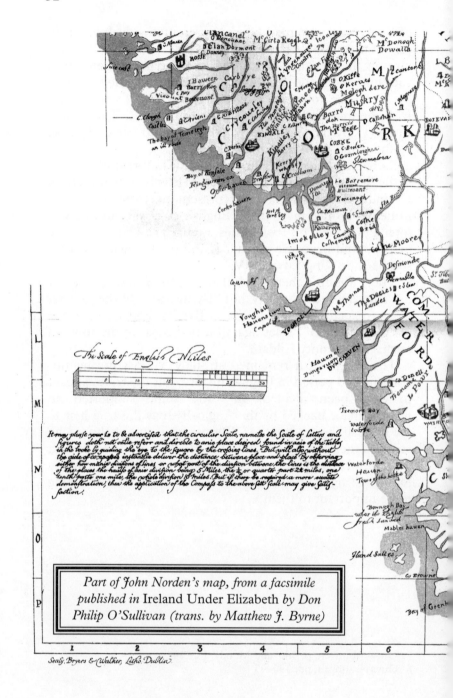

Sealy, Bryers & Walker, Litho. Dublin.

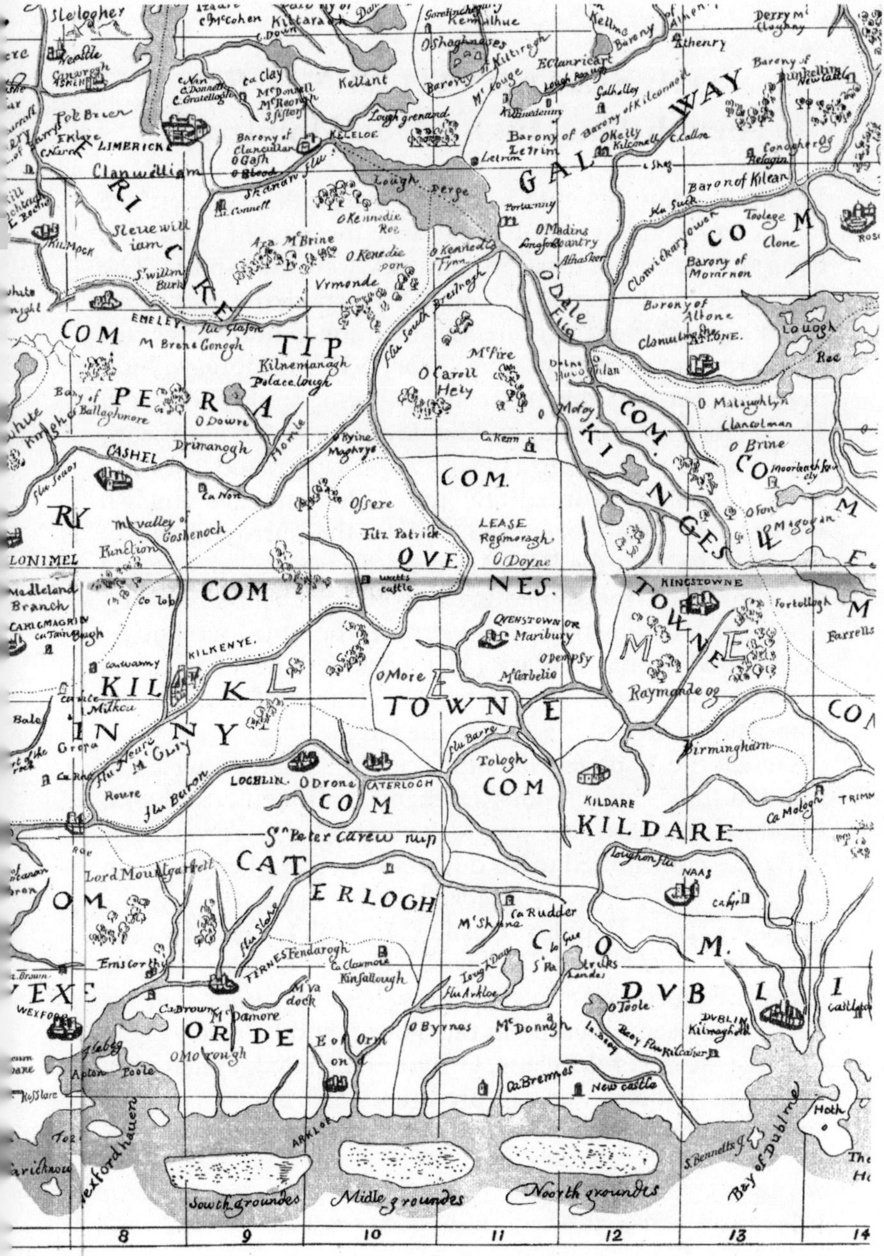

LIMERICKE
Clanwilliam
Kellant
Lough grenand
Barony of Clancullan
KELELOE
Lough Derge
Shanan flu
GAL WAY
Athenry
Barony of Kiltiragh
Barony of Kilcomoill
Baron of Kilean
Barony of Morarnen
Barony of Altone
ATLONE.
Lough Ree
O Kennedie Roe
O Kenedie Fynn
Vrmonde
O Carroll
Hely
M Brene Gonogh
TIP
PE RA
RY
Kilnemanagh
Polace lough
Drimanogh
CASHEL
Ossere
Fitz Patrick
QVE NES.
COM.
LEASE
Regmoragh
O Doyne
KINGSTOWNE
Fortollogh
QVENSTOWN OR Mariburry
O Dempsy
O More
TOWNE
KING'S TOWNE
O Malaughlyn
Clancolman
O Brine
Farrells
COM
KIL KENNY
KILKENYE.
Mc Gilpatricke
Raymonde og
Birmingham
LOCHLIN.
O Drone
CATERLOCH
Tologh
COM
KILDARE
KIL DARE
TRIMM
Sr Peter Carew
CAT ERLOGH
Lord Mountgarrett
NAAS
Mc Shane
DVBLIN
DVB LI
O Toole
Kilmaghoth
VEXE ORDE
WEXFORD
Ens Corthy
Mc Damore
O Morough
O Byrnes
Mc Donnogh
ARKLOE
New castle
Kilcasher
S. Bennetts
Bay of Dublinn
Hoth
Wexford hauen
South groundes
Midle groundes
Noorth groundes
8
9
10
11
12
13
14

CHAPTER 7

THE SIXTEENTH CENTURY
Feagh MacHugh of the Mountain

During the late fifteenth and early sixteenth centuries, the king's representatives in Ireland were the earls of Kildare, a departure from the usual in that they were Irish-born. The personality and prestige of Gerald Fitzgerald, the eighth earl and a supporter of the pretender mentioned in the previous chapter, were such that King Henry VII soon forgave him; in return, Fitzgerald kept Ireland peaceful until his death in 1513. His son, also named Gerald, became the ninth earl; but he was not as strong a person as his father, and wars and raids frequently erupted. By the 1520s effective English control had again been reduced to the surroundings of Dublin. "Beyond the Pale," as this area was called, became the expression for something outside of civilized society. Anglo-Irish landowners and townsmen became increasingly disgruntled about the black rents – bribes to be left in peace – which they had to pay to the clan chiefs, and their complaints reached the ears of the king.[1]

Gerald the Younger, the ninth earl of Kildare, traveled to London three times to answer charges of misrule, and with the third summons he was locked up in the Tower. The O'Byrnes contributed to his downfall in 1533 when Eamonn Og O Broin (O'Byrne) attacked Dublin and released the prisoners from Dublin Castle.[2] In 1534 Gerald's son Thomas, called Silken Thomas because of tassels which he and his cohorts wore in their hats, heard a rumor that his father had been executed in the Tower, and he rose against the king. Many of the clans, O'Byrnes included, joined him; but when Thomas was captured (and later hanged, drawn, and quartered), the revolt died out.

1. In medieval times, the word "mail" often was used to mean "rent." Thus our word "blackmail."
2. Moody, VIII, chronology for 1533.

To digress a moment, the O'Byrnes frequently made truces with the English of Dublin, and just as frequently broke them. Their warlike behavior was in part due to the memory of loss of their Kildare lands, but also because fighting and plundering was their traditional way of life. When they were not fighting the English, disputes within the tribe or fights with usually friendly neighboring tribes were common. Thus, the Four Masters noted that in 1500 Cahir O'Byrne, chief of his tribe, was killed by his own kinsmen; and in 1523 Hugh O'Toole, "the most celebrated of his tribe for hospitality and nobleness," was killed by the O'Byrnes. Later, in 1579, the Four Master's eulogy for Hugh O'Byrne, chief of Gabhall-Raghnaill, was that "he was the warlike opponent and plunderer of his English and Irish neighbors." High praise indeed.

To explain "Gabhall-Raghnaill": by this time the O'Byrnes were well along the road to splitting into two tribes. The junior branch had become increasingly independent from the senior, from which "the O'Byrne" had always been elected. By 1579 the Four Masters clearly distinguished between the O'Byrnes of Crioch Branach (O'Byrne Country), the senior branch with seat at Newry; and the O'Byrnes of Gabhall-Raghnaill, the junior branch with seat at Ballinacor in Glenmalure.

This was the era in which the *Leabhar Branach* or *Book of the O'Byrnes* was written, between 1550 and 1630. Encompassing four poem-books eulogizing the military prowess, liberality, quarrels, sickness and deaths of four generations of junior branch leaders, the book, unfortunately, has never been translated into English. Celtic culture was held together by bards, story-tellers, and poets, who held high rank in Celtic society and wandered freely from one great house to another, paying for their keep with their art. A well-written poem could ennoble, but it also could shred the character of a leader who slighted a poet or was less generous than expected.

Returning to our chronology, there are only a few mentions of the O'Byrnes in the histories of the first half of the sixteenth century. When Silken Thomas was executed in 1535 one presumes they must have made another peace agreement with Dublin; but in 1540 the Chief Justice, as the king's justiciar was now called, "plunged into the mountain fastness of Glenmalure in pursuit of the O'Byrnes."[3] And in 1542, Thady Oge (or Teige Og, Tadhg Og) O'Byrne, chief of the senior branch, made full submission to the English, forfeiting the castle and lands of Newcastle McKenyan.

An English document of the time sheds some light on the relative strength of the two branches: "O Birn L. of y branaght 60 h. 1 B. 88 kern. Redmond m'Shane of Gowllranel 8 H. 40 k."[4] This meant that the O'Byrne, lord of Crioch Branach, could provide 60 horsemen, one battalion of gallowglass (60 to 80 Scot mercenaries each with an assistant), and 88 foot soldiers; while Redmond MacShane, chief of the Gabhall-Raghnaill, could provide eight horsemen and 40 foot soldiers. These figures probably referred to the feudal levies which the Chief Justice could, in theory, demand from the O'Byrnes to do the king's work, so they would have been full-time military forces. The two branches could raise hundreds of part-time fighters, of course, whenever they had cause.

The gallowglasses were the Irish answer to English military superiority. They were Scots mercenaries trained in English-style fighting who contracted their services for a season. Over the years, numerous groups settled permanently in Ireland and, while some became peaceful, many continued to hire out their swords. Among these were the MacSweeneys of Donegal and a sept of the MacDonalds in Wicklow.[5]

Although the senior O'Byrne branch was the wealthier and larger of the two, its policy after 1542 was to stay on friendly terms with Dublin. A 1552 English report praised them, saying that, although they paid no rent to the king, they maintained at their own expense 120 gallowglass, 80 horsemen, and numerous foot soldiers to assist the Chief

---

3. Moody, III, 44.
4. Liam Price, "The Byrnes' Country in County Wicklow in the Sixteenth Century," Part I, *The Journal of the Royal Society of Archeology of Ireland*, (1935), p. 227.
5. Gerard A. Hayes-McCoy, *Scots Mercenaries in Ireland (1566–1603)* (Dublin & London: Burns, Oates, & Washbourne, 1937), p. 45.

Justice. In 1556 the O'Byrnes contributed 12 horsemen and 24 foot soldiers to an English expedition against the Irish of the north. Soon thereafter Brien, son of Teige Og (the O'Byrne), was appointed sheriff of "Birnes country," and in 1567 Teige Og was given a pension of the revenues of his country. The anglicization of Crioch Branach was almost complete.[6]

This was not happening back in the hills of Gabhall-Raghnaill, where Hugh MacShane was leading the junior branch in raids against the lowlands. Hugh raised the junior branch to prominence, or perhaps notoriety, as evidenced by a 1574 list of towns in Kildare paying him black rent. It was this Hugh whom the Four Masters praised (damned?) as the plunderer of his English and Irish neighbors. One must wonder if the senior branch was entirely spared; about this time the area called Cosha passed from control of the senior to the junior branch.

Teige Og died in 1578, and his nephew Dunlang became the last leader to be inaugurated "the O'Byrne". When Dunlang died just two years later, he was not replaced because war with the English had again broken out, and Crioch Branach was overrun by them.[7] Hugh MacShane had died in 1579, and his son, Feagh MacHugh, succeeded him as chief of Gabhall-Raghnaill. By the following year the junior branch was hard at war with the English, assisted by many members of the disorganized senior branch led by Gerald, another son of Teige Og. Many members of the senior branch were killed that year, 30 at Ennereilly alone, probably in the futile hopes of regaining their lands. However, not all members of the senior branch were anti-English. At least one family, the O'Byrnes of Kiltimon, supported the English side, and one of them captained an Irish contingent which fought against Feagh MacHugh.[8]

The Desmond war, so called after the earl of Desmond, one of the principal rebels, broke out in Munster in 1580, primarily because of rivalries between Anglo-Irish lords and

6. Price, pp. 227–28.
7. Ibid., p. 229.
8. Ibid., p. 230.

London-appointed bureaucrats. Leinster became involved partly because of religion. According to the Four Masters, in 1580 "James Eustace broke down his castles after having embraced the Catholic faith and renounced his sovereign (Queen Elizabeth I); so that war and disturbance arose on the arrival of Arthur Lord Gray in Ireland as Chief Justice. The Kavanaghs, Kinsellaghs, Byrnes, Tooles, Gaval Rannall, and the surviving inhabitants of Offaly and Leix, flocked to the assistance of James Eustace; so that the entire country from the Slaney to the Shannon and the Boyne to the Meeting of the Three Waters became one scene of strife and dissension. These plunderers pitched a camp on the confines of Slievroe and Glenmalure..."

James Eustace, the viscount of Baltinglass, had little success in his part of the uprising, except when he teamed with Feagh MacHugh in his mountain fastness. One of the first acts of the new Chief Justice, Lord Gray, was to disregard all advice and lead his imported army against Glenmalure. His first military action was almost his last, because his army was routed by the O'Byrnes (Baltinglass's forces were in reserve), and between 500 and 800 invaders killed. The victory sparked other uprisings throughout the country, and Feagh was assured of his place in history. In 1581 Feagh gave pledges to the government and was pardoned. He continued to rule a semi-independent Gabhall-Raghnaill. The Crioch Branach, however, never again shook off the English yoke.

Feagh returned to history's attention from time to time. In 1592 he gave shelter and assistance to Red Hugh O'Donnell, who had escaped from Dublin Castle. After O'Donnell recovered from near death through exposure – one of his fellow escapees did die – Feagh sent an armed escort to see him safely across the Liffey River. Later, Feagh sent men north to assist O'Donnell and O'Neill in their uprisings against the English. One group, led by Feagh's brother John, never returned to Wicklow and settled in County Louth to establish the O'Byrne line there.[9] In 1595

9. Patrick Kirwin, The Byrnes of County Louth," *County Louth Archaeological Journal*, II (1908–11), 46–49.

the Chief Justice led an army against Feagh at the request of his neighbors (the lowland Byrnes?), but Feagh and his followers escaped from their Ballinacor stronghold after a fight. The Chief Justice returned to Dublin and, in reprisal for the attack, Feagh's sons totally destroyed Crumlin, a town on the outskirts of Dublin.[10] The Four Masters noted that in 1596, "Fiagh, son of Hugh, son of John, from Glenmalure, was plundering Leinster and Meath."

Feagh was in frequent contact with the Ulster leaders during this period, sent men to their support as noted above, and on occasion requested help from them. In 1596 several contingents of Irish and gallowglasses sent from the north to help Feagh to maintain his insurrection were intercepted and defeated; but Feagh assured O'Neill that he would not make a separate peace. According to a letter which has survived, in 1596 Feagh informed O'Neill that he had asked O'Donnell to send him a company "of good shott for the guard of my bodie wheresoever I shall goe."[11] Feagh may have had some foreboding that his imminent death would be caused by a traitor from within his own family or followers.

Feagh was assassinated in May 1597 and, depending on which history one reads, his head either was sent to Queen Elizabeth I or spiked over the gates of Dublin. The Chief Justice was blamed for his assassination, but some historians suspect that it may have been an in-family settling of accounts, that the senior branch of the O'Byrnes was responsible.[12]

Feagh's two sons, Phelim and Redmond, carried on. At first they sought refuge in the north with O'Neill, who sent troops with them when they returned to the Wicklow mountains to continue the fight. For a brief period in 1598 they observed a request from other tribes who were negotiating with Dublin "to desist from their acts of plunder and rebellion," but later that year they were back at it. In

10. O'Toole, pp. 350–52.
11. Hayes-McCoy, p. 272, 278.
12. Liam Price, "The Byrnes' Country in County Wicklow in the Sixteenth Century: And the Manor of Arklow," Part II, *Royal Society of Archeology of Ireland* (1936), p. 60.

1599 Robert, Earl of Essex, sent 7,000 soldiers against Leinster forces which included the "Gaval-Ranall"; but Essex's general, Sir Henry Harrington, was defeated and many of his soldiers were killed, at Deputy's Pass near Wicklow, by the Irish commanded by Phelim O'Byrne.[13]

The following year Donnell Kavanagh, supposed king of Leinster, made peace, and the sons of Feagh also laid down their arms. English documents show, however, that in 1600 Lord Justice Loftus asked that 400–500 Scots highlanders be enlisted against the O'Byrnes, who were the occasion of considerable disturbance in their Wicklow fastness, because the highlanders would be well suited for mountain warfare.[14]

13. O'Toole, p. 398.
14. Hayes-McCoy, p. 373.

CHAPTER 8

THE SEVENTEENTH CENTURY
The English Prevail

The seventeenth century was to witness the final subordination of the Irish tribes by the Norman/English, a process which had required almost five hundred years to accomplish. By the beginning of the seventeenth century it was obvious that there was little hope of throwing off the English yoke; but the Irish continued to try, and there were to be two major wars before the century ended. The clan O'Byrne participation in the two, however, was no longer organized. Though many fought, especially in the mid-century War of the Confederation, they fought as individuals; clan leadership, in either branch, no longer existed.

After the Leinster tribes submitted in 1600–1601, English attention was concentrated on the north. Remote from Dublin and living in geographically protected terrain, the Ulster tribes always had been even more rebellious than those of Leinster. Years of constant warfare wore them down, however, and in 1607 the O'Neill, the O'Donnell, and one hundred of their principal lieutenants abandoned Ireland for the continent in what was to be called "the flight of the earls."[1] Their intention was to seek help from traditional enemies of England and then return; but few were ever to see Ireland again. The English were quick to take advantage of the leadership vacuum and massive land seizures occurred. These lands were parceled and sold to thousands of English and Scots Protestants in what was the beginning of the plantation system. Finally, after centuries of high costs and no profit, the English government had found a way to make money from Ireland, and it began looking for other lands to

---

1. The English king made the O'Donnell and the O'Neill earls of Tyreconnell and Tyrone in the expectation that they henceforth would be his vassals. English titles, however, meant nothing to the Irish, whose leaders were elected and not appointed. See p. 18, note 6.

confiscate. This soon led to the loss of much of the O'Byrne lands in Wicklow.

When Phelim MacFeagh O'Byrne made his submission to the Council of Dublin in April 1601, he extracted certain promises in return. In 1604 King James I confirmed that Phelim and his brother were the rightful owners of the lands formerly possessed by Fiagh MacHugh and, as long as James I lived, they enjoyed them undisturbed.[2] Covetous eyes were watching, however, and, following the king's death in 1625, several attempts were made to prove that Phelim, Redmond, and their sons were rebels. If so, their lands could be confiscated. They spent much time imprisoned in Dublin Castle while witnesses were threatened and tortured to testify against them. In 1628 their lands were forfeited and passed to others, primarily to one Sir William Parsons who had been the leading schemer against them. Phelim did not long survive this, dying in 1630. Two of his sons took service in the army of Spain, and the other three became ordinary members of the farming class. Thus the junior branch lost its leaders and its cohesion.[3]

The senior branch suffered multiple losses of its lands. In 1604 eighty O'Byrnes of this branch lost their lands for rebellious acts which had occurred 24 years earlier: support of Feagh MacHugh in 1580.[4] The remainder, already disorganized, fairly peaceful, and usually loyal to Dublin, still possessed most of the lands in 14 parishes along the coast of Wicklow between Delgany and Ennereilly. Sir William Parsons, not satisfied with the lands of the junior branch, approached the king's representative, Thomas Wentworth, Earl of Strafford, with a complicated scheme to prove royal title to the Byrnes' lands. Wentworth modified the plan to exclude Parsons, obtained the approval of King Charles I, and many of the remaining O'Byrne landowners were

2. Edge, p. 42.
3. J. P. Cooper, "Strafford and the Byrnes' Country," *Irish Historical Studies*, Vol XV No. 57 (March 1966), pp. 1–20.
4. John D'Alton, *Illustrations, Historical and Genealogical of King James's Irish Army List, 1689* (Dublin: 1855), p. 431.

dispossessed.[5] A 1641 survey showed that in 13 of the 14 parishes once owned almost entirely by the O'Byrnes, native Irish, mostly O'Byrnes, owned 19,900 acres while Protestants held 23,300 acres, 22,570 of which belonged to Wentworth and Parsons.[6]

These blatant confiscations through devious and questionable legal machinations were troublesome even to many Protestants of the day, but the lands were gone forever. The O'Byrnes had lost all political clout, those who had attempted to live in peace with the English had suffered as much as those who had not, and their resentment ensured that Wicklow would be a center of the rebellion to come.

The roots of the rebellion of 1641, one of the bloodiest in Irish history, were complex and many. Suffice to say that the O'Byrnes of Gabhall-Raghnaill were among the principal Leinster conspirators, especially Hugh MacPhelim, who had returned from Spain with his brother Brian. The rebellion was to begin with the seizure of Dublin Castle the night of October 23, 1641; but Hugh MacPhelim and his fellow raiders were betrayed a few hours before the attack. Simultaneous uprisings occurred, however, in Ulster where thousands of Protestants were slaughtered, and in Wicklow where, as one history put it, "those who dwelt in Ranalagh (anglicization of Gabhall-Raghnaill), anciently belonging to the family of the O'Byrnes, began likewise scabbadging the Protestants who lived among them ... from hence the flame spread to the O'Tooles and to the Byrnes who lived beyond the great water."[7]

The 1641 rebellion probably would have been short-lived had England not been in such turmoil. King Charles I could not send an army to Ireland without summoning a parliament to grant him the money; and his reluctance was proven correct when he did so some years later, and that parliament had him beheaded. For several years Ireland had been ruled by a

5. Cooper, pp. 1–20.
6. Ibid., pp. 16-17.
7. John T. Gilbert, ed., *The History of the Irish Confederation and the War in Ireland* (Dublin: 1862), Vol I, p. 23.

confederation – thus "War of the Confederation" – of Catholic peers who professed loyalty to the king while making demands which he was hesitant to approve. Protestants continued to hold a number of major cities and sporadic fighting occurred, with the O'Byrnes of Wicklow quite active in military and governmental affairs. In 1664 Edmond Birne, James Birne, and Bran Birne, captains in charge of 100 infantry each, were officers in a Confederation army sent to Ulster.[8] Brian Mac Phelim Byrne was a Leinster representative to the General Assembly. Phelim's other son, Colonel Hugh O'Byrne, was a prominent military leader in the Irish forces during this period.

Following the execution of Charles I in 1649, Oliver Cromwell turned his attention to Ireland. We have no record of how many Byrnes fell in his massacres, but they must have been many. Some 80 to 100 Byrnes subsequently were outlawed and their properties seized,[9] a great many in an era when Dublin itself had less than 20,000 inhabitants. The outlawries did much to complete the work of Parsons and Wentworth, and many of the Byrnes whose land ownership had survived the earlier confiscations were dispossessed. In 1641 Catholics still owned 41 percent of Wicklow; by 1688 this had been reduced to 14 percent.[10]

Other than a few almost illegible genealogies on microfilm in the Dublin Library, there are few indications of research on the dispersal of the O'Byrne clan after the War of the Confederation. Many probably remained in the Wicklow area as tenant farmers, while others moved elsewhere in Ireland to seek a livelihood. Some joined the "wild geese" to fight in the armies of Europe, and the family name appeared often on the military rosters of countries such as Spain, France, Germany, Austria, Poland, and Russia. In 1667, a Colonel Robert Byrne returned to Ireland under French auspices to rouse the country, but he was captured. In 1681,

---

8. Gilbert, III, pp. 202–03.
9. Ibid., pp. 340–49.
10. Moody, III, p. 368.

Colonel Denis O'Byrne was allowed to recruit 500 Irish to go to the Netherlands to fight for France.[11]

Denis O'Byrne returned some years later to join the Catholic cause in the Jacobite war of 1690–1691. Records of the losing – Jacobite – side were poorly kept. We know that at least 11 O'Byrnes were officers at the time of the Battle of the Boyne, thanks to a list composed by the French, and hundreds of others must have served in the ranks.[12] The clan O'Toole, with which the O'Byrnes were thoroughly intermarried, lost eleven of its members serving as officers at the battle of the Boyne, including one who commanded a regiment raised in Wicklow.[13] There is no record of how many O'Byrnes fell at the Boyne, at subsequent great battles such as Aughrim, or how many left for France with the defeated army after the final surrender at Limerick.[14]

Thus, in the course of one century a thousand-year-old clan was destroyed. Much of the disintegration occurred early in the century following the Wentworth-Parsons machinations to seize the Gabhall-Raghnaill and Crioch Branach lands. When most of the land remaining was confiscated after the mid-century War of the Confederation, those O'Byrnes who were not pushed west of the Shannon or into exile became tenant farmers on lands they formerly owned. The end-of-the-century Jacobite War was the final coup de grace to those few O'Byrne who still had hopes of clan revival. The name O'Byrne and its variations survives as one of the most common in Ireland but, regretfully, many of those who bear it have little knowledge of the role their forebears played in Ireland's long and sorry history.

11. Ibid., p. 599.
12. D'Alton, appendix.
13. O'Toole, p. 486.
14. A few, however, were identified in an October 8, 1691, letter from Jacobite commander Major General Patrick Sarsfield to Williamite commander General Ginkel. Sarsfield requested safe conducts for "Lt. Col. Birne, Capt. Charles Birne, Capt. Garrett Birne, Capt. John Birne, Lt. Peter Byrne, and Ensign James Birne" to return to their homes to collect their belongings, presumably to accompany Sarsfield to France. See appendix to J.T. Gilbert, ed., *A Jacobite Narrative of the War in Ireland 1688–91* (Dublin: 1892).

> *Reduced facsimile from* The History of
> the Clan O'Toole and Other Leinster Septs
> *by Rev. P.L. O'Toole*

No. IV.—THE GENEALOGY OF THE UI FAELAN.

(THE CLAN O'BYRNE.)

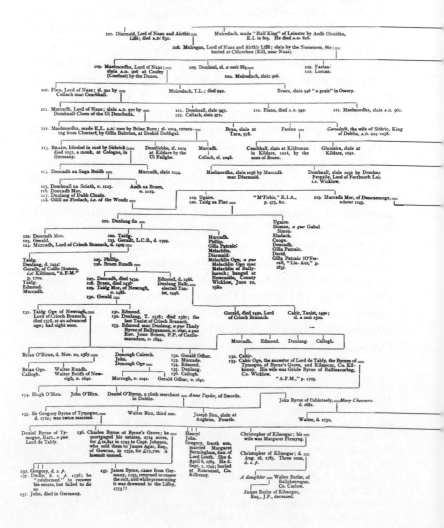

(SEQUEL TO THE UI DUNLANG.)

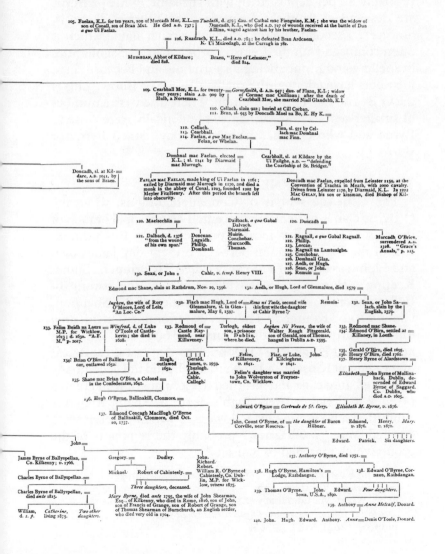

OTHER ORIGINS OF THE SURNAME BURNS

Probably 80 per cent of Irish with surname Byrne or Burns are descendent from the Leinster clan O'Byrne. There is, however, a second large group with similar name which is often confused with the Leinster sept because of similarities in spelling and pronouncing its surname, and because some members have adopted the spelling Byrne or Burns. This is the O'Beirne clan of Roscommon. There also were a number of smaller septs whose surnames phonetically were close to Byrne and whose descendants are today named Byrne or Burns.

THE CLAN O'BEIRNE

The O'Beirne sept is of Connaught origins, while the O'Byrne clan is of Leinster descent. The principal branch of the clan O'Beirne was located on the County Roscommon side of the River Shannon between present-day Jamestown and Elphin as chiefs of a territory called Tir Briuin na Sinna. Keating's *History of Ireland* places this in the barony of Ballintobber in the parishes of Kilmore-of-the-Shannon, Cloonaff, and Kilumed.[1] The clan was prominent in this area until the early seventeenth century. In 1601 "the" O'Beirne accompanied Hugh Roe O'Donnell to that last great defeat of the clans at Kinsale; but presumably he did not accompany Red Hugh into exile and returned to Connaught with Hugh's brother Roderick.[2] After Hugh's death in Spain, Roderick submitted, and among his followers to whom pardons were granted were "7 O'Birnes," probably the remnants of the group which marched to Kinsale.[3]

1. Geoffrey Keating, *The History of Ireland* (Kansas City: Irish Genealogical Foundation), Vol III, p. 735.
2. W. G. Wood-Martin, *History of Sligo, County and Town, from the earliest ages to the close of the reign of Queen Elizabeth* (Dublin: Hodges, Figgis and Co., 1882), Vol I, p. 365.
3. Ibid., p. 370.

In 1593 Queen Elizabeth granted lands in Roscommon to Terence O'Byrne, in fee.[4] These lands were in the parishes of Arcarne and Isertsnow in the barony of Boyle, which is quite close to O'Beirne country. It is probable that Terence O'Byrne was in truth Terence O'Beirne. Others of that surname had spread to adjoining baronies and across the Shannon to County Leitrim.

O'BIRN OF CARRA

The Book of Lecan, written about 1417, contains a topographical poem which describes the various land holdings in the Connaught territory of Hy-Fiachrach. A portion reads, "The lordship of O'Birn extends from the causeway of Cillin na n-garg to Beul atha na sesidh, Roibin beag being on the east side, and from Sighin Ciarain to Tobar Lughna." This is in the barony of Carra in southern County Mayo between Ballinrobe and Castlebar.

In his *Irish Families*, Edward MacLysaght said that a branch of the O'Beirne clan settled in Mayo north of Ballinrobe. In his book on the Hy-Fiachrach, John O'Donovan said that the name O'Birn was still common in that area (he was writing in 1844), but it had been anglicized to Byrne.[5,6]

O'CONBOIRNE OF ERRIS

In another portion of O'Donovan's book, reference is made to a family named MacConboirne, also called O'Conboirne, located in the barony of Erris in western County Mayo. O'Donovan footnotes that the name is now Burns, "which is a great corruption." Erris is a large area, but O'Donovan provided no further details about the family's location.[7]

4. John D'Alton, *History of Ireland: The Annals of Boyle* (Dublin: 1845), Vol I, p. 234.
5. John O'Donovan, *The Genealogies, Tribes, and Customs of Hy-Fiachrach* (Dublin: Irish Archeological Society, 1844), p. 159.
6. Edward Lysaght, *Irish Families, Their Names, Arms, and Origins* (New York: 1972), p. 54.
7. O'Donovan. *Genealogies*, p. 217.

O'BROIN OF KILLIAN

Also in Keating's *History of Ireland*, there is mentioned an O'Broin, anglicized Burns, who was chief of Lough Gealgosa, a district adjoining Corca Mogha. Corca Mogha comprised the parish of Kilkeeran in the barony of Killian, County Galway.[8]

MUINTER BIRN OF ULSTER

Another historical mystery is a group called the Muinter Birn of Ulster. An early mention of the Muinter Birn was in a 12th century manuscript of genealogies, now called Rawlinson B 502, which linked them with the tribe Sil Cuind. An article in *Irish Sword* describing tribal commitments to "the" O'Donnell circa 1350 said that the Muinter Birn were to provide 32 fighting men. The article placed the Muinter Birn in the southern part of the barony of Dungannon, County Tyrone.[9]

Keating's *History*, in describing the various MacSweeney septs, said that one was the MacSweeney Boghhamach which had a castle at Rathain in what is now the barony of Banach in County Donegal, and in whose territory was situated Reachrain Muintiri Birn, now called the Rathlin O'Beirne islands.[10]

These islands, or island, appear on present-day maps as Rathlin O'Birne Island. It was mentioned in the Civil Survey of 1654 thusly: "Parrish of Glancollmekill contains island called Raughrey Birne belonging to Thomas Lord ffoliott."[11] The harbor opposite the island was mentioned by the Four Masters in an entry for AD 1542 as called Reachrainn Muintire Birn in Tir Boghaine.

In 1835, O'Donovan commented on this area, "Many of the Connaught families have emigrated hither from the

---

8. Keating, III, 736.
9. Colm O Lochlainn, "O Domhnaill's Claims for Military Service," *Irish Sword*, V(1962), 117–18.
10. Keating, III, 725.
11. Robert C, Simington, ed., *The Civil Survey (A.D. 1654–1656)*, Vol III (Donegal, Derry, and Tyrone), Dublin, 1937.

opposite coast, as the O'Haras, O'Mallies, O'Birns."
O'Donovan also said O'Beirne is the name of a very
numerous family in the parish.[12] The Cromwellian census of
1659 had listed nine O'Birne families as living in the baronies
of Banagh and Boyloch.[13]

It is not clear whether these Donegal Byrnes, Birnes, or
Beirnes are descendent from the Muinter Birn of Tyrone,
which could have migrated west, or the O'Beirnes of
Roscommon. For that matter, O'Donovan's comment is
unclear. By "the opposite coast" did he mean the east coast,
e.g., Wicklow, or the coast of Sligo south across Donegal
Bay? This seems more probable because of his reference to
"Connaught families."

THE BOURNE(S) OF CASTLECONNOR

In 1655, Sir Richard Coote's Regiment of Horse of the
Cromwellian army, was disbanded in County Sligo, and land
seized from Catholics was distributed to the veterans. Among
these was one James Byrne (with variations in related
documents of E. J. Byrne and James Birne), who had been
the Quartermaster of Coote's Regiment. Byrne received a
grant of 1214 acres in the barony of Tireragh, which is where
Easky and Castleconnor are located.[14]

In 1689, Thomas Burne, tanner, of CastleCanur, County
Sligo, was listed on a James II Bill of attainder.[15] *The Bourne(s)
Families of Ireland*, written by a descendant, attributes the
origins of the Castleconnor branch of the Bourne family to
French Huguenots who were with Cromwell's army. The
book identifies as possible ancestors Thomas Burne of
Castleconnor, mentioned in a 1665 document, and James
Burne, mentioned in a 1678 document. The book does not

---

12. John O'Donovan, *Letters containing information relative to the Antiquaries
    of the County of Donegal. Collected during the progress of the Ordnance
    Survey in 1835* (Dublin: 1926).
13. Seamus Pender, ed., *A Census of Ireland circa 1659* (Dublin: 1939).
14. Wood-Martin, II, 92, 269, 175.
15. Mary A. Strange, *The Bourne(s) Families of Ireland* (The Stemar
    Corporation, 1970), p. 18.

connect the latter with James Byrne of Coote's Regiment, perhaps because the spelling of Byrne implies Catholic, albeit apostate, origins; but it is possible that James Byrne was the founder of the Protestant Bourne family of Castleconnor. An abandoned Catholic cemetery in Easky contains several tombstones with spellings Bourne and Bournes, however, which shows that spelling alone is not proof of one's family or faith.

OTHER AREAS OF IRELAND

Most of the above possibilities are from the northwest portion of Ireland (because that is where my particular Burns family resided and my research centered), and it is probable that there were many other small septs in other portions of the country whose names evolved as Byrne or Burns. For example, Rawlinson B 502 contains a genealogy of the "Clainne Birn" which was connected to the tribe Sil Aeda Allain, and a genealogy of the "Dail Birn" of Ossraige (Ossory).[16]

---

16. M. A. O'Brien, ed., *Corpus Genealogiarum Hiberniae* (Dublin: 1922).

GORMLAITH

There were two famous Gormlaiths in O'Byrne history, both of whom married three times, and each time well.

The first Gormlaith, who married into the clan, was the daughter of Flann Sinna, lord of the Southern Ui Neill and king of Meath. He also was high king of Ireland from AD 879 to AD 916. Gormlaith's first marriage was to Cormac, bishop-king of Cashel. This marriage was merely symbolic because Cormac maintained his celibacy. After Cormac was killed in 908 at the battle of Ballaughmoon in southern Kildare, Gormlaith married Cormac's slayer Cerball, lord of the Ui Faelain and king of Leinster; but Norsemen killed Cerball within the year leaving her widowed for the second time. The marriage did produce a son, Cellach, whose descendants became the Mac Fhaelan branch of the Ui Faelain which provided many of the tribe's kings before it died out in the late twelfth or early thirteenth century.

The *Annals of the Four Masters* preserves a poem composed by Gormlaith to commemorate her dead husband:

"There are nine kings of famous career, in a noble
   church of shining lustre,
Muiregan, hero without mistake, Cellach and Cerball
   the prudent,
Colman, Broen, and Bran the lively, Finn, Faelan,
   Dunchadh the bold;
In Cill-Chorbain, I have heard, their warlike graves were
   made."

Cill-Chorbain is the present-day Kilcorban in Ely O'Carroll, County Offaly. Why these early kings were buried so far from their Leinster capital at Naas, I do not know.

Gormlaith's third husband was Niall Glundub of the northern Ui Neill, high king of Ireland from 916 until killed by Norsemen in 919. Gormlaith lived on in her third widowhood almost 30 years, dying in a nunnery in 948.

The second famous Gormlaith, though perhaps "infamous" better describes her, was born shortly after her namesake died. She was the daughter of Murchadh, lord of the Ui Faelain and king of Leinster, who gave her as child bride to Olaf Cuaran ("Ironshoe"), the Norse king of Dublin and York. Gormlaith gave birth to his son Sitric when she was about 15 years old. In 980 Olaf abdicated the throne to Sitric's older half-brother and entered the monastery of Iona where he died the following year. Although divorces were possible under Brehon Law, and Gormlaith later was to experience one or more, she probably still was married to Olaf when he died. Soon after, Gormlaith became the wife of Maelsechlainn II, king of Meath and high king of Ireland. It is not clear what role Gormlaith played in the ascendancy of her brother Maelmordha to the Leister throne, which he obtained in 995 by killing the incumbent Dunchadh of the Ui Dunchadha, but her character was such that she could well have been involved. Gormlaith was, to say the least, a very strong-willed woman. In any case, she was too much for Maelsechlainn to handle, and he divorced her about 997. There is no record of any children. Sitric "Silkbeard," her son by Olaf "Ironshoe," had become king of Dublin when a servant killed his half-brother, and Gormlaith lived with him while attempting to instigate trouble for Maelsechlainn in revenge for having abandoned her.

In 999 Gormlaith met her third husband Brian Borhuma ("Cattle Tribute"), better known to history as Brian Boru. Brian was king of Munster and wanted to be high king. In 999 Maelsechlainn relinquished the southern half of Ireland to him, but Leinster's king Maelmordha and other Leinster princes were not in accord. The Leinster Irish and the Dublin Norse fought the armies of Brian and Maelsechlainn at Glenmama in Kildare, and they were defeated. Dublin was sacked and Sitric submitted. To seal the peace Brian gave Sitric a daughter in marriage, and Sitric (in revenge?) gave Brian his mother Gormlaith.

There is some uncertainty about the legalities. Brian had a living wife, which has led some scholars to suspect polygamy. Whatever, Brian and Gormlaith were married in the year 1000, and in 1002 a son Donnchad was born about the time Brian succeeded Maelsechlainn as high king. Years later, in 1023, Donnchad would become king of Munster after arranging for his half-brother Teigue to be assassinated.

The marriage between Gormlaith and Brian Boru must have been rocky, and its inevitable breakup led to the battle of Clontarf and the death of Brian. Shortly before, Maelmordha paid a royal visit to Brian and sister Gormlaith. His tunic, a gift from Brian,[1] had been torn in the journey, and he asked Gormlaith to repair it. Instead, she threw it in the fire and belittled her brother for having submitted to Brian, saying that neither their father nor grandfather would have. Still smoldering, Maelmordha was then insulted by Brian's son Murchadh, and he abruptly left for home in a rage. Brian sent a favorite page after him to attempt to placate him, but Maelmordha solidified the break in relations by killing the page. Brian thereupon sent Gormlaith back to her son Sitric in Dublin and began divorce proceedings.

Njal's Saga, an Icelandic epic composed soon afterwards, is one of the principal sources on the events leading to the battle of Clontarf. According to it, King Sigtrygg (Sitric) of Dublin sought the help of Earl Sigurd of the Orkneys to combat Brian Boru at the instigation of his mother Kormlod (Gormlaith), who was filled with hate for Brian and wished to see him dead because he had divorced her. The earl eventually agreed, on the condition that he would be given Gormlaith in marriage and would become a king in Ireland. Gormlaith then persuaded Sitric also to seek the help of the Viking Brodir whose fleet was anchored off the Isle of Man. Brodir extracted the same promise of marriage to Gormlaith and the kingship. Although Gormlaith must have been 60 years old at the time, the Saga described her as a most

1 In ancient Ireland a tribe paid tribute to its overlord, who acknowledged the tribute through a gift to the tribe's king. Brian had given Maelmordha a tunic.

beautiful woman who showed all the best qualities in all matters that were not in her power, but of an evil disposition in all those that were.

The battle of Clontarf was fought in 1014, and casualties were high. Neither Sigurd nor Brodir survived to claim the fair Gormlaith, Brian and two of his sons died, and Maelmordha also was killed. The Ui Faelain and its northern Leinster allies were so decimated that power in Leinster soon shifted to the southern Ui Cheinn Selaig alliance. Sitric survived and continued as king of Dublin for many more years. Maelsechlainn, who is believed to have kept his army nearby but neutral, again became high king and presumably kept far away from Gormlaith, though one must wonder what role she played when he was deposed in 1022.

The only subsequent mention of Gormlaith is in the Annals of the Four Masters under the year 1030:

> "Gormlaith, daughter of Murchadh, son of Finn, mother of the king of the foreigners, died.
>   'Gormlaith took three leaps,
>   Which a woman shall never take again,
>   A leap at Ath-Cliath, a leap at Taimhair,
>   A leap at Caiseal of the goblets over all'."[2]

There were few women in Irish history who influenced its course as much as did Gormlaith of the Ui Faelain. Daughter of a king, sister of another, mother of two, and wife to three, she more than anyone brought about the demise of the great Brian Boru, would-be unifier of Ireland; while at the same time lured to their deaths (albeit inadvertently) two of the principal foreign threats to Ireland – Sigurd, earl of Orkney, and Brodir the Viking – only to set the scene for a lengthier invasion of Ireland during the following century. The battle of Clontarf destroyed her own people, the Ui Faelain, and it was the king that the southern Leinster tribes put on the throne[3] who invited in the Norman-English.

2 Ath-Cliath (Dublin) was a reference to Olaf Cuaran, Taimhair (Tara) to Maelsechlainn, and Caiseal (Cashel) to Brian Boru.
3 Dermot MacMurrogh

GENEALOGIES

THE GENALOGY OF THE UI FAELAIN

1 Faelain – King of Leinster AD 728–738, son of Murtagh Mor
2 Ruaidri – King of Leinster AD 776–785, defeated the Ui Muiredaig at the Curragh in 782
3 Diarmaid – Lord of Naas and Airthir Liffe, died AD 831. His brother Muiredach was King of Leinster AD 808–829
4 Muiregan – King of Leinster AD 862–863, killed by the Norsemen
5 Maelmordha – Lord of Naas, slain AD 915 by the Danes. His brother Domhnall was King of Leinster AD 871–884, and his brother Cearbhall Mor was King of Leinster AD 885–909. From Cearbhall descended the Mac Faelan line
6 Finn – Lord of Naas, slain AD 927 by his cousin the son of Cearbhall Mor. His brother Broen was King of Leinster AD 943–947
7 Murcadh – King of Leinster AD 966–972, slain AD 972 by the Ui Dunchadha
8 Maelmordha – King of Leinster AD 1003–1014, killed at the battle of Clontarf. His sister Gormlaith was married in turn to Olaf Ironshoe, King of Dublin; Maelseachlainn, High King of Ireland; and Brian Borumha, also High King.
9 Bran – King of Leinster AD 1016–1018, blinded by Sitric Silkbeard, died AD 1052 in the monastery of Cologne. The name Ui Bhroin, to become O'Byrne, was taken from him.

THE GENEALOGY OF THE SENIOR BRANCH OF THE CLAN O'BYRNE

10 Doncadh na Saga Buidh (of the Yellow Hound)
11 Domhnall na Sciath (of the Shields), alive in AD 1115
12 Donchadha Mor
13 Dunlang of Dubh Cluain (Duveluain)
14 Oilill an Fiodach (of the Woods)
15 Ugaire – His brother Murrough Mor of Duncaemoge (Dun-Kevoge) founded the junior branch (see next section). It is not clear whether the clan split into senior and junior branches before the migration to the Wicklows (the geographical

separation into mountain and lowland sectors may have caused this), but the migration appears to have happened during the life of Oilill or Ugaire when Faelan Mac Fhaelain of yet another branch (see generation 5 above) was tribal king.

16 Taidg na Fiac (of the Ravens)
17 Dunlang Fin – the "Dounlyng" who was active against the English AD 1308–1310
18 Dunchadh Mor
19 Gerald – King of Ui Faelain, died AD 1398. Probably the Gerald who submitted to King Richard II in AD 1394
20 Murcadh – Lord of Crioch Branach, died AD 1429
21 Phillip
22 Braen Ruadh
23 Doncadh – died AD 1434. Probably the "Donat" whom in 1425 the English called "captain of his nation"
24 Braen – died AD 1436
25 Taidg Mor of Newragh – alive in AD 1486
26 Gerald
27 Taidg Og of Newragh – Lord of Crioch Branach, died AD 1578
28 Dunlang – nephew of Taidg Og. The last inaugurated head of the clan. Died AD 1580

THE GENEALOGY OF THE JUNIOR BRANCH OF THE CLAN O'BYRNE

15 Murrough Mor of Duncaemoge (Dun-Kevoge)
16 Doncadh
17 Ragnall – from whom Gabhall-Raghnaill is named
18 Phillip
19 Lorcan
20 Ragnall na Lamtuaighe (of the Battleaxe)
21 Conchobar
22 Domhnall Glas
23 Aedh (or Hugh)
24 Sean (or John)
25 Remuin (or Redmond)
26 Sean
27 Aedh – Lord of Glenmalure, died AD 1579
28 Feagh MacHugh – Lord of Glenmalure, killed May 8, 1597

SELECTED BIBLIOGRAPHY

The Annals of the Kingdom of Ireland, by the Four Masters. Ed. John O'Donovan. 7 vols. Dublin: 1848–71.

Berleth, Richard. *The Twilight Lords: An Irish Chronicle.* NewYork: Alfred A. Knopf, 1978.

The Burns Family in Ireland and America: The 1900 and 1901 Family History and Narratives of Patrick Burns. Ed. Richard N. Burns. Unpublished, 1988.

A Census of Ireland circa 1659. Ed. Seamus Pender. Dublin: 1939.

The Civil Survey (AD 1654–1656). Ed. Robert C. Simington. Vol III—Donegal, Derry, and Tyrone. Dublin: 1937.

Cogadh Gaedhel re Gallaibh: The War of the Gaedhil with the Gaill, or the Invasion of Ireland by the Danes and Norsemen. Trans. James H. Todd. London: Longmans, 1867.

Cooper, J. P. "Strafford and the Byrnes Country." *Irish Historical Studies,* XV, No. 57 (March 1966), 1–20.

Corpus Genealogiarum Hiberniae. Ed. M. A. O'Brien. Dublin: 1922.

D'Alton, John. *The History of Ireland: Annals of Boyle.* 2 Vols. Dublin: 1845.

—— *Illustrations, Historical and Genealogical, of King James's Irish Army List, 1689,* Dublin: 1855.

Edge, John. *The O'Byrnes and Their Descendants.* Dublin: Porteous and Gibbs, 1879.

The Genealogies, Tribes, and Customs of Hy-Fiachrach. Ed. John O'Donovan. Dublin: 1844.

Gilbert, John T. *The History of the Irish Confederation and the War in Ireland.* Dublin: 1882.

Hayes-McCoy, Gerard A. *Scots Mercenaries in Ireland (1565–1603).* Dublin: Burns, Oates, and Washburne, 1937.

A Jacobite Narrative of the War in Ireland, 1688–91. Ed. J. T. Gilbert. Dublin: 1892.

Keating, Geoffrey. *History of Ireland.* 3 Vols. Kansas City, Missouri: Irish Genealogical Foundation, 1983.

Kirwin, Patrick. "The Byrnes of County Louth." *County Louth Archeological Journal,* II (1908–1911), 45–49.

Landon, Michael. *Erin and Britannia: The Historical Background to a Modern Tragedy.* Chicago: Nelson-Hall, 1981.

Leabhar Branach: The Book of the O'Byrnes. Ed. Sean MacAirt. Dublin: The Dublin Institute for Advanced Studies, 1944.

MacLysaght, Edward. *Irish Families: Their Names, Arms, and Origins.* New York: Crown Publishers, 1972.

Moody, T. W., F. X. Martin and F. J. Byrne, eds. *A New History of Ireland.*
Vol II: Medieval Ireland (1169–1534). Oxford: 1982.
Vol III: Early Modern Ireland (1534–1691). Oxford: 1976.
Vol VIII: A Chronology of Irish History to 1976. Oxford: 1982.
Vol IX: Maps, Genealogies, Lists. Oxford: 1984.

Njal's Saga. Trans. Carl F. Bayerschmidt and Lee M. Hollander. New York: New York University, 1955.

O'Byrne, Clarinda Mary. *Historical Reminiscences of O'Byrnes, O'Tooles, O'Kavanaghs, and other Irish Chieftains.* London: M'Gowan, 1843.

O'Donovan, John. *Letters Containing Information Relative to the Antiquaries of the County of Donegal: Collected During the Progress of the Ordnance Survey in 1835.* Dublin: National Library of Dublin, 1926.

O Lochlainn, Colm. "O Domhnaill's Claims for Military Service." *Irish Sword.* V (1961–2), 117–18.

O'Toole, P. L.. *The History of the Clan O'Toole and Other Leinster Septs.* Dublin: 1890.

Orpen, Goddard Henry. *Ireland Under the Normans, 1169–1216.* Oxford: Clarendon Press, 1968.

Otway-Ruthven, A. J. *A History of Medieval Ireland.* New York: St. Martin's Press, 1968.

Price, Liam. "The Byrnes' Country in County Wicklow in the Sixteenth Century." *Journal of the Royal Society of Antiquaries of Ireland.* Part I (1933), Part II (1936).

Ryan, John. "The Battle of Clontarf." *The Journal of the Royal Society of Antiquaries of Ireland* (1938).

Simms, J. G. *Jacobite Ireland, 1685–91.* Toronto: University of Toronto Press, 1969.

—— *The Williamite Confiscation in Ireland, 1690–1703.* London: Faber & Faber, 1956.

Strange, Mary A. *The Bourne(s) Families of Ireland.* The Stremar Corporation, 1970.

Smyth, Alfred P. *Celtic Leinster: Towards an Historical Geography of*

Early Irish Civilization A.D. 500–1600. Dublin, Irish Academic Press, 1982.

Wood-Martin, W. G. *The History of Sligo, County and Town, from the Earliest Ages to the Present Time.* 3 Vols. Dublin: 1882–92.